Dedicated to Billy Graham,
who has shared the love of
God with so many

Copyright © 1992 by Patricia Richardson Mattozzi
First published in 1992 by Derrydale Books
distributed by Outlet Book Company, Inc.,
a Random House Company,
40 Engelhard Avenue
Avenel, New Jersey 07001

Manufactured in the United States

Designed by Melissa Ring

Library of Congress Cataloging-in-Publication Data
Mattozzi, Patricia.
God is love / by Patricia Richardson Mattozzi.
p.   cm.
Summary: Illustrated selections from the Old and New Testaments.
ISBN 0-517-08143-1
1. God—Love—Juvenile literature.   [1. Bible—Selections.]
I. Title.
IN PROCESS   92-12769
231'.6—dc20   CIP
AC

8 7 6 5 4 3 2 1

God is Love

Patricia Richardson Mattozzi

Derrydale Books
New York • Avenel, New Jersey

For He shall give His angels charge over thee,
to keep thee in all thy ways.

PSALM 91:11

Teach me your ways, Lord; make them known to me.
Teach me to live according to your truth.

PSALM 25:4

When I am afraid I will
ut my trust in Thee.

PSALM 56:3

The Lord is my rock, and my fortress, and my deliverer;
my rock in whom I take refuge.

PSALM 18:2

I rejoiced when I heard them say let us go
into the house of the Lord.

PSALM 122:1

Go therefore and teach all nations,
baptizing them in the name of the
Father, the Son, and the Holy Spirit.

MATTHEW 28:19

Let everything that has breath praise the Lord.

PSALM 150:6

A friend loveth at all times.
PROVERBS 17:7

Thy word is a lamp unto my feet and a light unto my path.

PSALM 119:105

The wolf will live with the lamb, the leopard will lie down with the goat, the calf and the lion and the yearling together; and a little child will lead them.

ISAIAH 11:6

Blessed are the peacemakers

for they shall be called the children of God.

MATTHEW 5:9

I love you, O Lord.
PSALM 18:1

Unto Thee, O God, do we give thanks.

PSALM 75:1

Are we not all children of one Father?
Did not one God create us?

MALACHI 2:10

Let us love one another.

JOHN 15:17

Open Thou mine eyes, that I may behold wondrous things.

Rest in the Lord.
PSALM 37:7

The earth is the Lord's
and the fullness thereof;
the world, and they
that dwell therein.

PSALM 24:1

Thou art my hiding place and my shield.

PSALM 119:114